WILD IRIS

Blooms May through July. The iris, also known as the Rocky Mountain Iris or Western Blue Flag, grows a large, delicate, blue-violet flower with darker blue-violet veins. You will find it in moist meadows and along stream banks growing in dense clumps and flowering as the soil begins to dry with summer's arrival.

COLUMBINE

Blooms June through August. The Blue Columbine is a bushy plant. It grows up to three feet tall and produces many showy flowers. The center of the flower is yellow and has five white petals, called sepals, around it. The larger petals are pale blue to dark blue and have delicate spikes pointing away from the flower's front side. You will find this plant growing near aspen groves and rocky slopes.

BITTERROOT

Blooms May through July. The Bitterroot is a low-growing plant. Only after its leaves appear and then die do the flowers begin to bloom. This plant grows on the Western Slope on rocky mesas and open places near sagebrush or pines. The genus (or family name), Lewisia, was named in honor of the Lewis and Clark Expedition. Captain Meriwether Lewis was the first to collect this flowering plant.

PRICKLY PEAR CACTUS

Blooms May through June. This plant grows in clumps low to the ground. It has lovely yellow flowers and mean, prickly spines or needles. Because it is a cactus, it likes to live in open areas in very dry soil. Be careful where you step!

PAINTBRUSH

Blooms May through September. This plant is also called Indian Paintbrush or Wyoming Paintbrush. When this flower is in bloom, you will see that it looks like someone dipped the flower into a bucket of red paint. It grows one to two feet tall in mountain meadows.

INDIAN PAINTBRUSH AND SNEEZEWEED

Blooms May through September. Paintbrush come mostly in red shades that blend into their green stems. There are also yellow paintbrush called Sulfur Paintbrush. The sneezeweed is not the prettiest plant around, but it has a fun name. It is a great concern to sheep ranchers because it is highly poisonous for sheep.

WILD ROSE AND IRIS

The wild rose grows all over the country. The red berry it makes in the fall is called a "hip." In the fall, the green leaves of the rose plant turn reddish/brown. The iris looks alot like the iris you may find in your neighborhood. Most of the wild iris are blue to purple. A few are yellow.

BLUE LUPINE

Blooms June through August. The lupine belongs to the pea family. You will find them in open fields and among the pine trees. Lupine come in blue, purple, light blue, or yellow. As the plant matures, you may find pea pods where flowers once were.

MULE'S EARS

Blooms May through July. This plant is part of the sunflower family and grows west of the Continental Divide. It can grow up to three feet high. In large bunches, it can cover an entire field like a golden carpet. The large, bright-yellow flower has a raised center. Its large, hairy leaves give the plant its name because they are shaped like a mule's ear.

SNEEZEWEED

Blooms July through September. This plant is called Owlclaws, Helen's Flower, and Yellow Star, but the name "Sneezeweed" started when people realized that this plant could make you sneeze! Sneezeweed has yellow/orange flowers and grows on western slopes where there are wet mountain meadows.

TWINFLOWER

Blooms June through September. This tiny plant grows leaves in small clusters close to the ground. Two pink flowers with white tips are produced on straight stems only about four inches tall. It grows in moist evergreen woods in peatmoss, and where it is cool.

HAREBELLS

Blooms June through September. The Harebell is also called Bluebell or Bluebell of Scotland. These blue-violet flowers hang like a bell from a slender stem. This plant can grow taller than three feet. At elevations near timberline, it may only be four inches tall. It is a hardy plant and grows in bunches on rocky slopes and high mountain meadows.

SUNFLOWER

Blooms late summer. The Common Sunflower is also called the Kansas Sunflower. This sunflower has bright yellow petals and a dark brown-to-black center. It grows in the foothills and can be seen along roadsides. In good conditions, it will grow six feet tall.

MULE'S EARS AND STICKY GERANIUM

Blooms May through August. Mule's Ears have large yellow flowers and leaves that grow taller than its flower. It will completely cover an open field if left undisturbed. The Sticky Geranium is also known as the Crane's Bill. It is a common weed with pink flowers and a seed pod that is long and pointy like a Crane's beak.

PASQUEFLOWER

Blooms March through April. Also called Wild Crocus or Lion's Beard. The Pasqueflower is in the buttercup family. It has white or blue-violet petals and silky hairs over its leaves and stem. It can grow up to one foot tall. The flower appears before the leaves do.

SEGO LILY

Blooms May through July. Sego Lilies, also known as Mariposa Lilies, grow in clusters of showy, white to violet, bell-shaped flowers that have a yellow center and dark, reddish-brown markings that circle the center. This plant grows ten to eighteen inches tall in dry soil near aspen groves and mountain meadows.

STICKY GERANIUM AND MOOSE

Blooms May through August. The Sticky Geranium, or Crane's Bill, has hairy red-tinged stems, and green leaves that grow near the ground. A cluster of pink to purplish flowers grow in clusters. It grows in woods and meadows from the foothills to the mountains.

FIREWHEEL AND CREEK

Blooms May through July. The Firewheel is also called Indian Blanket and is part of the sunflower family. It grows about two feet high. The petals have a deep, red-orange color with bright yellow on the outer tips. The head, or center, of this flower is deep red-brown with some yellow, and very prickly to touch.

ROSE

Blooms May through July. The Nootka Rose is a thorny bush that has small, light-pink flowers. This wild rosebush will grow to over ten feet high if it likes where it is growing. The flowers are only two to three inches wide. In the fall, the base of the flower turns into a red berry, or rosehip. This berry can be made into tea.

COLORADO BLUE COLUMBINE

Blooms June through August. This graceful, showy plant produces several delicate flowers at a time with white petals surrounding a yellow center, and long, pointy sepals behind the petals. There is also a yellow columbine that appears similar to the blue columbine, but prefers a sheltered, moist growing area.

FAIRY SLIPPERS

Blooms March through July. Fairy Slipper, also called Calypso, is part of the orchid family. The reddish stem supports a delicate, pink-purple flower that resembles a slipper. At eight inches tall, it is difficult to find where it grows, hidden in the cool, dark, and moist areas of forests.

SHOOTING STAR

Blooms April through August. There are several species of Shooting Stars. The one pictured above is called a Dark-Throat or Few-Flowered Shooting Star. It is a delight to discover, growing in moist mountain meadows and along stream sides. The clusters of bright-pink flowers expose a white and then yellow ring around the dark center which points downward like a bird beak.

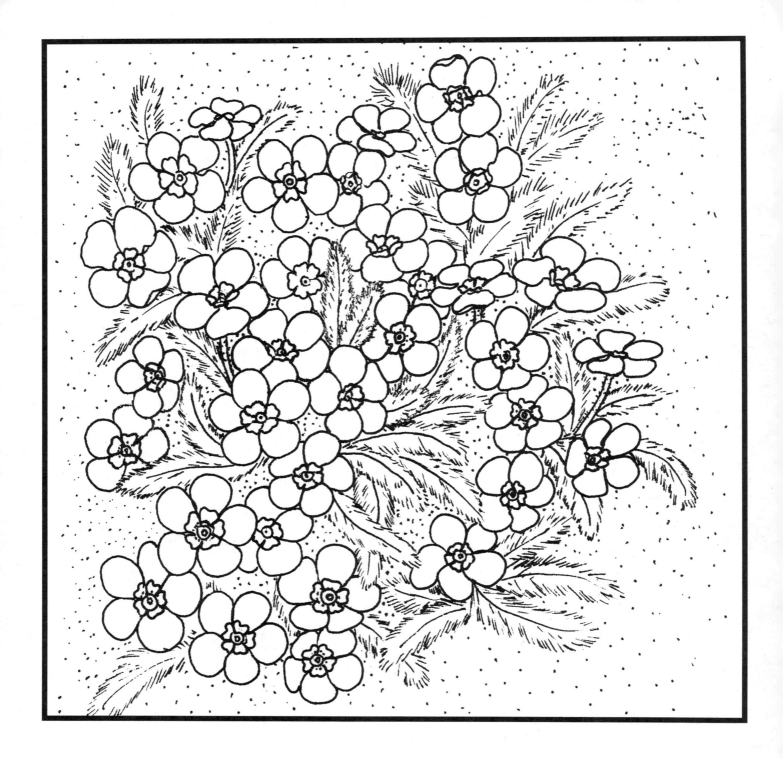

FORGET-ME-NOT

Blooms June through August. This delicate looking, low growing plant is quite hardy. It lives high in the mountains on rocky slopes. The deep blue petals come from a bright, yellow center. The leaves are covered with long hairs, and give them a wooly look.

BUNCHBERRY

Blooms June through August. The Bunchberry grows from two to eight inches high. It has many tiny greenish flowers at its center, and the four white "petals" around it are called bracts. The leaves, bracts, and greenish flowers grow on a short stem. You will find this plant in moist, wooded areas.

BUTTER-AND-EGGS

Blooms July through September. Also called Common Toadflax. The Butter-and-Eggs flower got its name because of its coloring. This plant has very bright-yellow flowers with a warm orange color in the middle area that sticks out like a lower lip. It grows in thick bunches along roadsides or in fields.

LARKSPUR

Blooms March through July. The Upland, or Nuttall's Larkspur, is a showy plant with deep-blue to purple flowers. The flower projects backward on its stem like a spur. It grows about one and a half feet tall. It can be found in dry. and moist areas of the mountains. In the spring, it is poisonous to grazing cattle.

BOG LAUREL: *TOP LEFT* The Bog (or Alpine) Laurel has bowl-shaped, deep-pink flowers and grows in wet mountain meadows or bogs, which is how it got its name. Its height may vary from four to twenty inches. BLUE-EYED GRASS: *TOP RIGHT* Blooms April through September. Blue-Eyed Grass is a member of the iris family. It usually has one flower blooming at a time, and the flower opens only when the sun is shining. The petals are a deep purple-blue color with deeper-colored stripes. GLOBEFLOWER: *BOTTOM RIGHT* The Globeflower has many names, including Butterball. This plant will grow to nearly two feet tall. It has light, creamy-yellow flowers in the shape of a globe. BUTTERCUP: *BOTTOM LEFT* This buttercup, known as the Subalpine Buttercup, has very shiny, deep-yellow petals. It grows in the mountains on rocky slopes or meadows. Buttercups are considered poisonous.

STORKBILL: *TOP LEFT* The Storkbill is a member of the geranium family. The leaves are small and fern-like. The flower's petals are a rosy color. When the petals fall, the seeds look like the bill of a stork, which is how the plant got its name. **MONKSHOOD:** *TOP RIGHT* The flowers of Monkshood are similar to the Larkspur, however the Monkshood plant will grow much taller. Monkshood actually has a hood on the top part of the flower and that is why this plant has its name. **MONKEYFLOWER:** *BOTTOM LEFT* There are several kinds of Monkeyflowers. The petals are mostly orange to pale-yellow with reddish spots near the center of the flower. **ELEPHANTSHEAD:** *BOTTOM RIGHT* The many pink-to-reddish flowers that grow on the stem of this plant look quite like a pink elephant! The trunk is easy to spot. If you look closely, you will also see elephant ears.

MATCH-UPS
Which group of flowers is not like the other? (see answer on last page)

Help the hummingbird find the flower.
(see answer on last page)

T	P	O	R	K	G	N	U	C	S	I	P	W
R	E	W	O	L	F	B	J	M	X	W	L	O
G	T	I	B	E	N	I	B	M	U	L	O	C
K	A	L	O	A	P	T	H	O	T	D	A	P
M	L	D	N	V	R	J	A	D	O	W	D	B
P	H	F	O	E	I	O	Q	C	O	O	V	U
E	T	L	C	S	C	L	S	O	R	R	I	N
I	X	O	I	T	K	B	I	E	R	G	O	C
H	M	W	T	L	L	O	D	T	E	I	W	H
U	Q	E	Z	U	Y	A	E	M	T	F	L	B
P	I	R	I	S	P	V	M	E	T	S	Z	E
G	D	A	L	L	E	O	C	P	I	Q	U	R
O	Y	H	U	P	A	E	H	A	B	U	L	R
Z	L	U	D	O	R	W	D	J	O	R	D	Y

Find the words below in the boxes above and circle them.
BITTERROOT, BUNCHBERRY, COLUMBINE, FLOWER, GROW, IRIS, LEAVES, LILY, PETAL, PRICKLY, PEAR, ROSE, SEED, STEM, WILDFLOWER (see answer on last page)

WILD WILDFLOWERS! A Story.

Once upon a _____ (noun) in the Rocky Mountains, there lived a _____ (adjective) flower called Sneezeweed. This _____ (adjective) flower was once a _____ (adjective) plant. It loved the _____ (season) when the _____ (adjective) sun shone down on it all day. Then one day it saw _____ (plural noun) coming to admire it. The Sneezeweed was so _____ (adverb) of itself. When the _____ (plural noun) bent down to _____ (verb) its flower, they sneezed! The flower became all _____ (adjective) and its petals started to _____ (verb). Ever since then, this once _____ (adjective) flower became known as Sneezeweed!

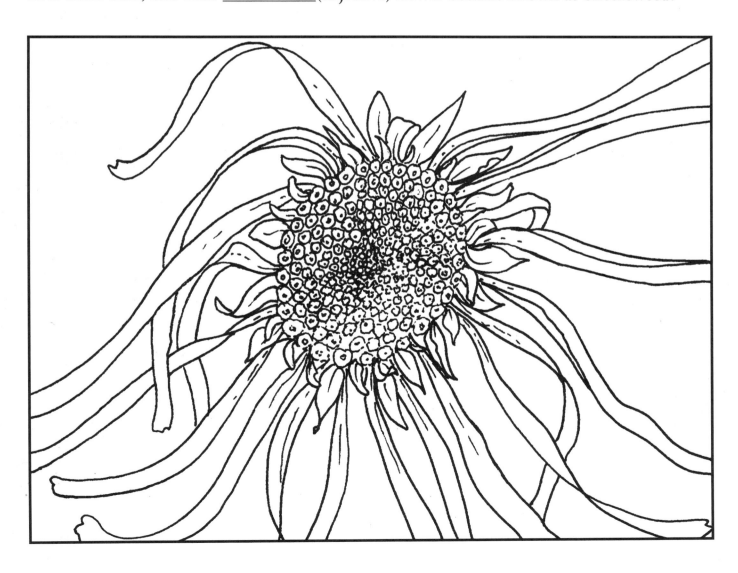

PINK to RED:
* Rose
* Bitterroot
* Bog Laurel
* Elephantshead
* Paintbrush
* Storkbill

RED/VIOLET:
* Shooting Star

PURPLE/BLUE:
* Blue-Eyed Grass
* Columbine
* Harebell
* Iris
* Larkspur
* Monkshood
* Pasqueflower

YELLOW:
* Butter-and-Eggs
* Buttercup
* Globeflower
* Monkeyflower
* Mule's Ears
* Prickly Pear
* Sneezeweed

WHITE:
* Bunchberry
* Sego Lily

COLOR INDEX
for all pages

ANSWER PAGE

The group of flowers in the upper left is not like the others.
The flower on the left has no double edge on its petals.

MAZE

WORD FIND

Selected Bibliography

Coates, Margaret Klipstein. *Perennials for the Western Garden* (Pruett Publishing Co., 1976).

Guennel, Hilde E. *Guide to Colorado Wildflowers, Plains and Foothills* (Westcliffe Publishers, Inc., 1995).

Houk, Rose, text. *Wildflowers of the American West, A Photographic Celebration of Nature's Beauty* (Chronicle Books, 1987).

Johnson, Lady Bird, and Lees, Carlton B. *Wildflowers Across America* (Abbeville Press, 1988).

Line, Les, Editor of <u>Audubon</u> magazine, and Hodge, Walter Henricks. *The Audubon Society Book of Wildflowers* (Harry N. Abrams, Inc., 1978).

Miller, Millie, and Nelson, Cyndi. *Painted Ladies, Butterflies of North America* (Johnson Books, 1993).

Nelson, Ruth Ashton. *Plants of Rocky Mountain National Park* (Rocky Mountain Nature Assn. in cooperation with National Park Service, U.S. Department of the Interior, 1970).

Pesman, M. Walter. *Meet the Natives, A Beginner's Field Guide to Rocky Mountain Wildflowers, Trees and Shrubs*, 8th ed. (Pruett Publishing Co., 1988).

Peterson, Roger Tory, and McKenny, Margaret. *A Field Guide to Wildflowers of Northeastern and North-Central North America* (Houghton Mifflin Co., 1968).

Schreier, Carl. *A Field Guide to Wildflowers of the Rocky Mountains* (Homestead Publishing, 1996).

Spellenberg, Richard, Professor of Biology, New Mexico State University; Rayfield, Susan; and Nehring, Carol, visual key. *The Audubon Society Field Guide to North American Wildflowers* (Western Region) (Alfred A. Knopf, Inc., 1992).

Svolinsky, K., illustrations, and Barton, J.G., text. *Wild Flowers* (Spring Books, UK, 1964).

Venning, Frank D., and Saito, Manabu C., illustrations. *Wildflowers of North America, A Guide to Field Identification* (Golden Press, 1984).

Waidhofer, Linde, photography, and Lito Tajada-Flores, text. *High Color, Spectacular Wildflowers of the Rockies* (Western Eye Press, 1987).

Wells, Diana. *100 Flowers and How They Got Their Names* (Algonquin Books of Chapel Hill, 1997).